The Intangibles of Success

A Coaching Guide for Managers,
Mentors and Coaches, as well as a
Self-Directed Guide for Employees on
the Intangible Characteristics of
Professional Success

By Mary Kemmer

ISBN 978-0-578-13797-1

Intangibles – Contents

Introduction to Mary Kemmer and her Research

I have been coaching employees at all levels in various types of organizations— professional services, hospitality, financial services, and manufacturing—for many years.

At First Chicago (JP Morgan Chase) I coached individuals primarily on performance issues and advised those who were losing their positions due to downsizing.

As a Consultant at Marriott International, I transitioned into Leadership Development and coached high potential employees who were preparing for promotion to executive levels.

For the last 14 years, with Baker Tilly, LLP, I have continued coaching executive leaders, as well as high potential employees. Additionally, I developed curriculum and training programs to teach others how to coach.

In my years of coaching, I questioned what makes people successful. More importantly, why do technically strong people sometimes fail to reach top levels of organizations?

I began a research project focused on employees who were successful at the companies I had worked for to identify their common characteristics. Then I took the opposite approach and studied employees who were not successful, even though they had excellent to superior technical and managerial abilities. This began my personal project on understanding and defining the Intangible Characteristics of success.

- My **first** observation was that employees in the top tiers of organizations are not just <u>technically strong</u>. Many competent and accomplished technicians fail to reach the top levels.

- My **next** observation was that while many highly successful employees have <u>technical talent</u> and may also possess <u>management abilities</u>; some still fail to move successfully to the top levels of their organizations.

- I concluded from these observations that successful executives, in addition to being technically competent, generally have qualities that differentiate them from their peers who do not make it to the top. I started referring to these characteristics as "intangibles" and was on to a clearer way of describing and articulating these characteristics and what differentiates employee success.

In this book, I define Six Intangibles that are important for success and how this information will serve both Coaches and Professionals:

1. As a Coach or Manager, you will be able to provide better feedback and coach subordinates on the meaning and importance of intangibles in their careers
2. As an Employee, you will become aware of your intangible strengths <u>and</u> deficiencies by reading the case studies and completing an honest self-assessment regarding these six characteristics

The book describes intangibles and provides case studies, exercises and sample questions to generate coaching conversations. As you read through the material, use the case studies and exercises to heighten self-awareness. Use the Individual Development Plan to take action on the intangibles important for success in your career progression.

A Preface to Intangibles

There are four ways, and only four ways, in which we have contact with the world. We are evaluated and classified by these four contacts: what we do, how we look, what we say, and how we say it.

--Dale Carnegie

Perception is reality.
-- Anonymous

Over many years of managing and coaching executives and aspiring executives, I have observed how individuals develop, grow and move forward in their careers. I have also observed how they lose momentum, stall, and derail or fail to achieve their highest desired career goals.

Achieving a successful career requires technical competence as a foundation. Mastering the technical areas within a person's discipline is essential for career progression. Technical competence requires continuous learning, refining, and honing of our craft. We need to become respected as experts; highly regarded as managers, teachers and mentors; sought out for our knowledge. Technical knowledge is the tangible competency that we must achieve in order to attain middle and higher levels of management. At some point, however, "intangibles" become important differentiators of who will move into the highest levels of leadership. By "intangibles" I mean those qualities and characteristics not necessarily measurable but important, and essential for success into higher levels of organizations.

This book describes Intangible Characteristics and behaviors and provides guidance to coaches and employees alike.

For Coaches

Using the Intangibles Book

In successful organizations, managers effectively coach their people and work to develop them. It is every manager's responsibility to coach and professionally develop their direct reports. Imagine in the world of sports, if coaches saw their role as standing on the sideline, watching the field activity and then post-game criticizing the errors. For many managers this is their approach to coaching employees. There are a number of reasons why managers do not effectively coach their employees:

- Perhaps they don't understand the role of a coach in the business world.
- Maybe they were never formally trained to coach or don't have the skill or feel comfortable coaching.
- Or they may believe that if performance problems are ignored, they will go away.
- Or unfortunately, they lack the desire to coach or grow their people

In each of these situations there are ways to teach and support managers to become effective coaches. The benefits of coaching and developing your people are in the best interest for you, your business and your direct reports.

What are the Characteristics of a Good Coach?

I would like you to recall a great coach, leader or teacher you were exposed to as a young teen or adult and take a few moments to think about the characteristics that person possessed. How did they provide you with feedback, both positive and negative? How did they motivate you? How did they inspire you to become your very best?

Some of the behaviors of effective coaches, bosses, leaders and mentors that I have observed include:

- Recognizing that coaching is probably the most effective development tactic to grow their people
- Clearly stating expectations, timelines and goals before beginning a project or job
- Delegating work of substance, not just menial tasks, that will stretch their employees,
- Using mistakes as opportunities for learning and teaching
- Telling the truth—good and bad without demeaning the employee but with learning as the end result
- Describing their own personal successes and failures and lessons learned
- Sharing their stories and challenges on the path to becoming a Leader
- Listening to employees' challenges and providing insights and solutions from a "seasoned" viewpoint
- Reinforcing the employees' strengths and working from their strengths to minimize weaknesses
- Treating their employees with respect and developing a relationship with them
- Developing an "Emotional Bank Account" with each employee (see page 32)
- Giving praise
- Leaving their people better, stronger and smarter than when they were first assigned to them

How this book will develop and support Coaching Skills

The book provides resources and techniques for coaching employees on understanding and strengthening intangible characteristics. Most managers do not have the confidence, instincts or technique to comfortably address intangibles because they are often personality, behavioral or character traits. And because coaching with regards to intangibles is often not dealt with in a straightforward manner, this book provides managers with tools to support their coaching efforts.

Mishandled coaching on intangibles can complicate or damage the coach-employee relationship. This book is intended to raise the coach's awareness of intangible characteristics and increase their confidence in coaching. It will also provide ideas to support coaches on how to coach appropriately and keep the employee on-track without compromising their relationships.

For Employees

Self-Awareness, Development, and Change

As you read this document, you will have an opportunity to clearly understand intangible characteristics and why they are important to your success. Chapters 1 and 2 are particularly important as they provide definitions and case studies that demonstrate intangible missteps.

We urge both employees and coaches to read the case studies. The employee should complete the self-assessment sections to identify their intangible strengths and development needs. By honestly answering the questions in each of the six intangibles areas, you will gain insight and self-awareness. Suggestions will be provided on how to validate and clarify development needs around intangibles and create a plan to strengthen them.

It is highly recommended that the employee meet with the Coach or Manager after completing these exercises. Because intangibles fundamentally refer to behavioral change, it is important to get support from those who work closely with you and can directly observe your behavior on an on-going basis.

Discussing your goals with your Coach, Manager or Mentor and soliciting support and feedback is extremely important in this process. Bring your main development points to your Coach and be candid and forthcoming in sharing self-observations by asking for feedback, validation, suggestions, ideas and support.

Chapter 1

Tangibles vs. Intangibles

What are "Intangibles" and how do they differ from tangible competencies?

- Tangibles are generally competencies and skills, and usually concrete, measurable, and definable.

- Intangibles are characteristics, behaviors, and personal attributes which may be hard to measure, hard to define, and difficult to discuss in a straightforward manner. They pose a unique challenge for effective coaching.

In clarifying and differentiating these terms with regards to professional success, we have included the term competency to describe tangibles, and characteristic when referring to intangibles.

Tangible Competencies

Tangible competencies are easier to define than intangible ones. Here are some examples:

1. Tangible competencies might include technical skills, such as computer skills, negotiating skills, project management, or strategic planning.

2. Tangible competencies are the skills necessary for success in one's occupation. For example, a Physics Professor would be expected to have the education, depth and knowledge of the field of Physics.

3. Tangible competencies may also refer to the required credentials to be qualified for a position. For example, an accountant needs to have knowledge of tax laws and eventually pass the CPA exam.

4. Tangible competencies can include skills that define the roles and responsibilities of a position. For example, successful consultants need to be skilled in project planning and management.

5. Tangible competencies are used in job descriptions to describe the job's roles and responsibilities. They are generally used for setting performance goals as they describe measurable work. For example, a Training Manager would be expected to create training curriculums and provide training workshops and would be measured on those skills during the performance review.

EXERCISE 1 for the COACH and EMPLOYEE

List the key tangible competencies required for success in your current position:

1. _____

2. _____

3. _____

4. _____

5. _____

The Six Intangible Characteristics

What are intangible characteristics?   Below is a list of intangible characteristics considered highly important for professional success:

- Being in **Alignment** with the philosophy and strategy of the company or organization and fitting into its culture

- Having **Advocates** to support your career success

- Demonstrating **Integrity and Trust**

- Being **Organizationally Savvy**

- Developing and sustaining strong **Relationships and Networks—Internally and Externally**

- Displaying **Professional Image and Presence**

Intangible characteristics are more difficult to define and discuss because they focus on aspects of individual behavior, character or personality, not skills, credentials, or competencies. They are also difficult to measure because of their qualitative, not quantitative nature. They may often be perceptual, meaning that they are based on what people see and perceive, not necessarily on who you are. But perceptions can contribute to your professional reputation.

Intangibles present a complex coaching challenge in that they are sensitive and require greater thought, reflection and feedback to comfortably discuss. There are generally no easy training remedies for developing desirable intangible characteristics. For example, you cannot attend a workshop to become organizationally savvy. Organizational savvy requires awareness, understanding of your environment and commitment and support to change.

NOTE ON YOUR PROFESSIONAL REPUTATION

How do you change negative perceptions or a negative reputation? Time and a serious commitment are required to change negative perceptions. To turn your reputation around, SOLICIT and ACCEPT feedback, be OPEN to change, have a clear UNDERSTANDING of what needs to change and request ongoing feedback. You will need to work closely with your Coach.

Chapter 2

Six Intangibles Characteristics That Support Career Success

Chapter 2 provides a clear, step-by-step process for both Coaches and employees to understand and discuss intangibles and their importance for success.

The case studies provide real examples of real situations told in real words to showcase relatable scenarios.

The self-assessment questions start the employee on the path to self-awareness and can also be used as a format for discussion between the coach and employee. The exercises can be used individually, with a coach or with the boss. When used with the coach or boss, the exercises provide a framework for an honest, open dialogue; individually the exercises create self-awareness and a framework for creating an individual development plan.

> *We are measured not by who we are, but by the perception of who we seem to be; not by what we say, but how we are heard; not by what we do, but how we appear to do it.* ---Anonymous

Intangible Characteristic 1:

Being in Alignment

The case studies presented in this book are based upon situations observed in years of coaching employees.

The first case study provides insight into what "being in <u>alignment</u> with the culture of the company" means. The higher you move into an organization the more important it is to think of senior management as your professional teammates. Alignment is "fit". Fit can be defined as: do I like you; do I fit into this team; do I wish to make this team successful? Alignment is important in both directions—the employee needs to feel aligned to the organization and the organization needs to perceive the employee as aligned.

The following exercises will support the Coach and Employee in clarifying the employee's existing alignment with the culture, the philosophy of the company, and the actions required to change the perception of non-alignment. The case study and following exercises provide examples for discussion when coaching the employee.

Case Study on Alignment:

Sam holds the position of Marketing Manager for a division of a large retail company. By all appearances, Sam has the right stuff to move into executive management. He is well credentialed, well educated, technically creative, and very bright—in fact, one of the company's brightest managers. Additionally, he has executive bearing and looks the role—tall, slender, handsome, and impeccable. On the surface, he seems like someone you would be proud to have represent your company.

When I first met Sam, he was very ambitious, ready to move ahead, but it wasn't happening. I interviewed him and asked him what he thought he needed to do to be considered for promotion. Sam was at a loss; he thought he had demonstrated all the tangible competencies required to be an executive. He was a producer and a rainmaker. But Senior Management did not consider him to be promotable—now or probably ever. Why? You see, managements' perception of Sam was that he was not aligned with the management goals or philosophy of the company. Why was he seen in this way? Sam had a tendency to verbally and sometimes publicly, and not diplomatically, disagree with management decisions—he was inappropriately critical on a number of policy changes and vocal in a number of meetings. Sam thought he was being honest; top management saw him as critical, lacking discretion and not supportive of the company and management's position.

Sam: I don't want to have to be a phony and "kiss up" to be successful. I want to be able to express myself.

EXERCISE 2 for the EMPLOYEE

Complete the following questions to determine to what degree you are aware of the importance of Alignment in your career.

Rate yourself on a scale of "1" to "5" on the following questions: "1" being low, indicating you may not be aligned; up to "5" being high, indicating you are aligned with the culture.

Do you respect Executive Management?	1	2	3	4	5
Can you say of the Executive Team, "I like and trust them?"	1	2	3	4	5
Do you relate well to your boss?	1	2	3	4	5
Do you support the company's strategy and the decisions of top management?	1	2	3	4	5
Do you promote and live by your company's core values? In both words and actions?	1	2	3	4	5
Are you capable of holding your tongue when you disagree with management until you have processed the "what's" and "why's" and thought out a diplomatic approach to discussing it?	1	2	3	4	5
Are you perceived as being in sync and supportive of the thinking of your leadership?	1	2	3	4	5

Are you optimistic about Executive Leadership, policies, practices and future strategy of the company?	1	2	3	4	5
Do you work to promote camaraderie?	1	2	3	4	5
Are you committed to the company and its future?	1	2	3	4	5
Do you agree with the philosophy and values of Executive Management? Do you support the policies and values of the company in discussion with your peers and direct reports?	1	2	3	4	5
Does the Executive Management team know and respect you?	1	2	3	4	5

Notes on Alignment:

EXERCISE 3 for the EMPLOYEE

Having read the case study and answered the questions, define what alignment means to you personally:

How aligned are you with the values and policies of your company? Note: No organization is perfect. Only you know the personal values that are important for you to respect your company and its leadership.

How can you personally demonstrate alignment? What behaviors indicate that an individual is aligned with the culture?

EXERCISE and DISCUSSION 4 for COACH and EMPLOYEE

Having read the case study and completed the self-assessment, discuss the results with your Coach. Together, list two actions you could take right now to strengthen and demonstrate your alignment with the company:

1. _____

2. _____

Intangible Characteristic 2:

Having Advocates to Support Your Career Success

An Advocate is an individual who is at a higher level in your organization who respects you, your work, and supports your career success. They know the quality of your work and freely promote and support you when speaking to their Senior and Executive Management peers. An Advocate may provide support as a mentor and advisor. An Advocate can influence your professional reputation as they have direct access with their peer level.

Advocates cannot be gained by direct request! You must earn the respect of a potential Advocate by doing exceptional work, having professional exposure and contact over a period of time.

Case Study on Advocacy:

Laura was the Chief Financial Officer (CFO) for a medium-sized professional services firm. Laura was hired into the position a year ago, with previous experience as a CFO for a privately held organization. Laura was an intellectual. She had a superior mind and was a great problem solver. Initially Laura "wowed" everyone with her technical expertise and intellectual capabilities. In the first year in the position, Laura established solid relationships with her staff. She was well respected and trusted by them. But Laura failed to take the time and challenge to meet and establish relationships with the senior management of the firm. She preferred to operate mainly one-on-one with those junior to her. As a result, the Partners and Senior Managers never developed the kind of relationship with her to develop trust and credibility. They didn't know her beyond occasional presentations to the Executive Committee. She eventually derailed despite her technical abilities because she did not have advocates at the senior level.

Laura: I do my job, I know I am competent, why does work have to be so political?

Complete the following questions to determine to what degree you are aware of the importance of Advocacy in your career.

Answer the following questions by rating them on a scale from "1" to "5" with "1" being low, indicating little or no awareness of advocacy and "5" being high, indicating you have advocates in your company.

Do you have champions, advocates, or known supporters--meaning those at higher levels who know, respect and want to support your success?	1	2	3	4	5
Have you built rapport with the decision makers in your organization as well as the support staff and those at your level?	1	2	3	4	5
Do you relate to people in a way that is deeper than just the day-to-day transactions?	1	2	3	4	5
Do you have the respect and trust of your superiors?	1	2	3	4	5
Have you developed trust and credibility with your peers and direct reports?	1	2	3	4	5
Do you relate well to all kinds of people? At all levels?	1	2	3	4	5

	1	2	3	4	5
Do you have an advocate who will stand by you and support your continuous professional development and career progression?	1	2	3	4	5
Are you comfortable with higher management? Can you present comfortably to a group of executives without undue tension?	1	2	3	4	5

Notes on Advocacy:

After reading the case study and answering the questions, list advocates you currently have. Ask your coach to provide feedback as well.

Do you have an advocate?

Who would you like to have as an advocate?

Discuss with your Coach two actions you can take today to begin establishing relationships that will lead to gaining advocates in your company:

Example:

With your Coach, review your department's organization chart and identify two senior managers to introduce yourself to over the next few months. Discuss with your Coach how you will introduce yourself and the purpose for meeting. Remember this is part of your public relations strategy to expose yourself to high level managers and develop relationships with them that may eventually lead to advocacy.

1. _____

2. _____

ADDITIONAL THOUGHTS ON ADVOCATES

Goal for the Coach: To understand the importance of an employee having advocates who will publicly support and promote them.

What is an advocate? Why are they important? How do you gain the support of an advocate?

First, let's define the difference between a mentor and an advocate. Mentors will support you in your development, teach you skills, and provide advice. An advocate, however, is an individual at a senior level who respects and understands your skills and talents. Advocates are in a position to support and promote you to the decision makers in the organization.

Gaining an advocate can occur in several ways. You may want to create a strategy for developing a relationship that eventually becomes an advocacy relationship. Some ways that an advocacy relationship can develop might include:

- Through a coach or mentor who knows your work and understands the contribution you are making
- Through high-profile work where senior folks can observe and recognize your contribution
- Through a personal Public Relations campaign where you will ensure those who need to know are aware of the good work you are doing

Most people would just prefer that good, hard work be recognized without having to advertise (most think of talking about accomplishments as bragging.) You need to find ways to communicate to the appropriate people and in appropriate ways about the successes you have had. Communicating your successes can be formal or informal. You must be comfortable communicating and find your own style.

Some ways of communicating without bragging might include:

- Including successes as part of a status report when meeting with your boss
- Sharing accolades that are received from clients or internal folks by adding a note, such as, "I was happy and proud to receive this for the team" (make it humble)
- Volunteering for projects or community events that will provide you with face-time with senior members of your organization
- Taking the initiative to request one-on-one time (coffee or a brief meeting) with a senior member of the company to interview them on:

  - How they grew in their careers
  - How they developed a specific competency
  - Their development suggestions for someone at your level in the company
  - How they keep informed and what they read
  - The outside organizations or community groups they belong to
  - You might share an idea you have had to improve business and ask for their opinions, etc.

EMOTIONAL BANK ACCOUNT

A Useful Concept

Stephen Covey in, in his best-selling book <u>The Seven Habits of Highly Successful People</u> describes the concept of the "Emotional Bank Account." The "Bank Account" represents the building of a relationship by making "deposits" into a bank account of trust and friendship. He contends that there are six major deposits:

- Understanding the Other Person
- Attending to the Little Things in the Relationship
- Keeping Commitments
- Apologizing Sincerely When You Make a Withdrawal from the Joint Bank Account
- Clarifying Expectations Going Forward
- Showing Personal Integrity and Respect

In addition to deposits, there are withdrawals. If the "Bank Account" is well funded by deposits, the withdrawals will never bankrupt the relationship.

Intangible Characteristic 3:
Demonstrating Integrity and Trust

Integrity and trust are the foundations of all successful personal and professional relationships.

Case Study on Integrity and Trust

Allen was a project manager for a consulting firm. Colleagues and management respected his knowledge and work ethic. As a result, Allen was assigned to work on one of the highest profile projects with one of the firm's best clients. While working on this project, Allen became privy to sensitive information regarding a potential merger of his client with another competitor. At dinner one evening with his wife and some personal friends, Allen mentioned that there was a significant change about to happen in a company he was working with and that the work was interesting and challenging. It was just an innocent comment. However, his friends probed, asked questions and then guessed who the client was. Inadvertently, Allen had exposed confidential insider information. Although the information was contained (the client and the firm never found out), Allen had broken the confidential covenant that exists between a client's information and the Firm.

COMMENT:
This is one example of breaking trust. While Allen did not intentionally break trust, his boss and the client would have perceived him as doing so had they known of his disclosure.

Lack of integrity is a potential "career killer" and can take on many forms, from padding your time and expense reports to directly or inadvertently sharing confidential information. This type of behavior will have management questioning your integrity and honesty, or even considering termination.

EXERCISE 8 for the EMPLOYEE

Complete the following questions to determine to what degree you are aware of the importance of Integrity and Trust in your career success.

Answer the following questions by rating them on a scale from "1" to "5" with "1" being low, indicating you need to rethink your trustworthiness and "5" being high, indicating you believe you have high integrity and trust.

Do you follow through on your commitments?	1	2	3	4	5
Are you as good as your word?	1	2	3	4	5
Do you live a life inside and outside of work that is honest, decent, and honorable?	1	2	3	4	5
Do you use discretion in sharing information?	1	2	3	4	5
Do you use appropriate discretion with peers and subordinates regarding confidential or sensitive information?	1	2	3	4	5
Do you keep confidences?	1	2	3	4	5
Do you have an allegiance to your company?	1	2	3	4	5
Do you respect others?	1	2	3	4	5
Are you respected at all levels in the organization?	1	2	3	4	5

	1	2	3	4	5
Are you sensitive to making "withdrawals" from your emotional bank account with peers, subordinates or management?	1	2	3	4	5
Are you sensitive to making "deposits" into your emotional bank account with peers, subordinates or management?	1	2	3	4	5
If you have damaged a relationship, are you quick to apologize and make repairs?	1	2	3	4	5
Do you gossip?	1	2	3	4	5

Notes on Integrity and Trust:

EXERCISE 9 for the EMPLOYEE

After reading the case study and answering the questions, define what trust means to you.

- Are you behaving in a manner that displays trust and integrity?

- Do you need to increase your awareness of how you handle confidential information? Think in terms of all communications with friends, colleagues, direct reports, etc.

COACH DISCUSSION

Review Exercises 8 and 9 with the employee. Discuss honestly how the employee is perceived in the organizations and if this is an area of concern for their future growth.

ADDITIONAL THOUGHTS ON DEMONSTRATING TRUST AND INTEGRITY

Trust and integrity are the foundations for building professional relationships.

How is trust developed?
How do I demonstrate integrity?
Why will people trust me?

BEHAVIORS OF TRUSTWORTHY PEOPLE:

- They understand the other person's viewpoint, concerns, problems and issues
- They empathize with them
- They respect the ideas, position, status and needs of others
- They are genuine, open and authentic in their interactions
- They are predictable and consistent in what they say and do

ESSENTIAL BEHAVIORS FOR MAINTAINING TRUST:

- Keeping confidences
- Being prudent with sensitive information
- Following through on promises and commitments
- Acting with integrity
- Speaking favorably of colleagues, publicly and privately
- Giving time and energy to developing and sustaining your relationships
- Giving positive affirmation to another's ideas when they are good (publicly) and providing honest feedback if you disagree (privately)

- Honestly confronting conflict and trying to resolve it in a "win-win" way
- Sharing information that is valuable for your colleagues' success
- Respecting your colleagues in both words and actions

Intangible Characteristic 4:

Being Organizationally Savvy

The following case study is only one example of organizational savvy. People who are organizationally savvy generally understand how to get things done within the complexity of organizational structures and within the complexity of personalities. They act with discretion and thereby protect their credibility and reputation.

Case Study on Organizational Savvy:

Brian is an Assistant Vice President at a commercial banking company. Brian has been working at the bank for 3 years. He is very social and has developed relationships with many people at various levels in the bank. Brian has been working on policy changes regarding the upcoming year's benefit changes. The policy draft was finally completed and ready for review by the Executive Committee. Brian wanted to strengthen his relationship with Jim, a Senior Vice President, as he had considerable power and influence in the bank. Brian set up a lunch with Jim and shared a copy of the policy draft with him. Unfortunately, the draft ended up with an Executive Committee member and Brian had to explain his inappropriate actions.

Comments:

Brian was not being respectful of the organizational protocols. By not following communication protocols, he stepped on an Executive Committee member's toes. He acted with questionable integrity and organizational savvy. He broke an unspoken commitment. He didn't consider the impact of his actions and he caused political problems by not following established procedures.

Complete the following questions to determine to what degree you are aware of the importance of Organizational Savvy to your career success.

Answer the following questions by rating them on a scale from "1" to "5" with "1" being low, indicating a need to be more aware of your ability to understand and act appropriately in organizations and "5" being high, indicating you have organizationally savvy.

Do you accept that politics are a reality in most organizations?	1	2	3	4	5
Do you respect your superiors?	1	2	3	4	5
Are you sensitive to and aware of individual egos and territories?	1	2	3	4	5
Do you know the proper protocols and sequences for communicating information?	1	2	3	4	5
Does senior management trust you?	1	2	3	4	5
Are you persuasive with senior management?	1	2	3	4	5
Can you read the "climate" of groups and individuals as you work with them?	1	2	3	4	5
Do you make adjustments to accommodate "climate" changes when you see them occur?	1	2	3	4	5

Do you think about the ramifications of who, what, when, and how you share important communications before you do so?	1	2	3	4	5
Do you provide "previews" of information to those who need to know prior to meetings so there are no uncomfortable surprises? And do you provide an opportunity to revise or edit the information before it becomes public?	1	2	3	4	5
Do you know who to rely on to get things accomplished in your department? In other departments? In the Company?	1	2	3	4	5
Do you communicate in an honest manner that is the least controversial and provides the least "noise"?	1	2	3	4	5
Are you sensitive to the actions and reactions of others?	1	2	3	4	5

Notes on Organizational Savvy:

EXERCISE 11 for the EMPLOYEE

Having read the case study and answered the questions, define what Organizational Savvy means to you:

What answers were low on the scale, indicating that you should consider creating an action plan?

List two actions you can take to be become more Organizationally Savvy. For example:

- Use discretion with confidential information.
- Be aware of protocols. Who currently knows? Who needs to know? Share information in the order of protocols and the hierarchy.
- Be sensitive to sharing information in meetings that may not be for general distribution.

1. _____

2. _____

NOTES ON EMOTIONAL INTELLIGENCE

What is Emotional Intelligence (EQ)?

IQ is an abbreviation for your Intelligence Quotient. EQ represents your Emotional Quotient. Emotional Intelligence is your ability to understand other people, what motivates them and how to work cooperatively with them. High emotional intelligence will support your ability to be organizationally savvy.

Key EQ behaviors include:

- Not being swept away with anger and emotion and reacting without thinking
- Taking a "timeout" before responding to situations where you disagree or have passion
- Managing your emotional reactions without letting them overwhelm you
- Knowing your feelings and using them to make life decisions you can live with and that are in your best interest
- Reading other people without having them tell you what they are feeling
- Reading the "pulse" of a group
- Handling emotions in relationships with skill and harmony

http://www.talentsmart.com/about/emotional-intelligence.php

HOW TO BECOME ORGANIZATIONALLY SAVVY

Politics exist and are a part of most professional organizations. The following information contains tips to help you become more politically and organizationally savvy:

COMMUNICATE

- Determine who needs to know and what they need to know.
- Determine the order in which they should be informed; who needs to know first, second and so on.
- Do status reporting.
- Keep all the appropriate people in the loop.
- Share information with people outside the loop appropriately, if required or if requested.

DISASTER REPORTING

- Give management a "heads-up" on problems before they become a disaster and especially if there has been a disaster.
- Don't burden senior management with excessive, superfluous details and constant updates.
- Be succinct and top-line oriented—use the "Executive Briefing" technique to provide relevant information.

PICK YOUR BATTLES

- Seek advice on how to handle sticky situations from those who are organizationally savvy such as your coach, mentor, advocate or trusted advisor.

DEVISE A PUBLIC RELATIONS PLAN FOR YOURSELF

- Share your work accomplishments formally and informally through your networks by voice mail, e-mail, or written reports.
- Invite colleagues to get to know you and your work on a more personal level.
- Develop business relationships with key influencers in the company; make a targeted list of influencers to meet over the year.
- Identify a mentor to work with you formally or informally.
- Identify role models—people you respect. Study and emulate their behavior.

PROFESSIONALISM

- Understand the business of those with whom you interact.
- Understand the structure of the organization and the protocols and hierarchy.
- Understand reporting relationships.
- Identify the decision makers and get to know them.

RESPECT OTHERS

- Be respectful of all employees, regardless of level in the organization.
- Never bad-mouth your manager, management, company policies or practices.
- Understand and respect the agenda of others.
- Recognize all who contributed to a successful project.
- Share the stage with other contributors.
- Review important announcements with all those who need to know before going public.
- Never take credit for another employee's ideas or work.

Intangible Characteristic 5:

Developing and Sustaining Strong Relationships and Networks—Internally and Externally

Many professionals establish close relationships with a few peers and managers, never realizing the value and power of creating a broader network of contacts. As you add contacts, you broaden your professional reputation.

Case Study on Developing and Sustaining Relationships:

Robert was hired as a Director in a growing Information Technology company. When he first came on board he met colleagues in his department. He had good relationships with his immediate circle of employees but did not meet folks outside his group. After six months, he felt he was acclimated to the Company; however, he had a very narrow exposure to other departments and employees. After nine months, he became more and more insular. He didn't network with others outside of his department because his department had become his comfort zone. Robert didn't have relationships with the leaders of the company. He wasn't known well enough to have a professional reputation. Several years passed and Robert was not considered for a promotion.

Robert: I don't really understand why I haven't been recommended for a promotion. My Vice President gives me above average reviews.

EXERCISE 13 for the EMPLOYEE

Complete the following questions to determine to what degree you are aware of the importance of Internal and External Relationships to your career success.

Answer the following questions on a scale from "1" to "5" with "1" being low, indicating you may need to work on managing relationships and networking and "5" being high, indicating that you are well networked inside and outside of your organization. This exercise will help make you aware of your networking skills.

Have I taken the opportunity to meet people outside my department?	1	2	3	4	5
Do I know who the "influencers" are in the various groups? Other departments? Other offices, the Company?	1	2	3	4	5
Do I have a strategy to meet new people?	1	2	3	4	5
Do I have a mentor? Or informal mentor?	1	2	3	4	5
Do I attend after-work functions and mix with individuals I don't know rather than remain in my safety zone of people I work with?	1	2	3	4	5
Do I participate in meetings?	1	2	3	4	5
Do I have advocates—individuals at a higher level—who know and respect my work?	1	2	3	4	5

Having read the case study and answered the questions, why is it important to develop a network and relationships? How will it benefit you?

Notes on Internal and External Relationships:

Discuss your ratings in this section with your Coach. Together, discuss how to create a focused action plan to network and meet new people. Use your company directory or organization chart to highlight individuals you intend to introduce yourself to over the next six months. Select one person to invite to lunch or coffee every two weeks.

NOTE ON TRIANGLES IN RELATIONSHIPS

The "triangle" communication concept is a simple and effective method to incorporate into your relationship strategy. This communication model advocates that people speak directly to one another, not indirectly through three-sided triangles.

When hearing information from a third party about a second party, encourage party number three to speak directly with party number two. Information tends to get muddled, distorted and inaccurate when it is delivered second or third hand. The triangle is a hazard and can negatively impact one's career, integrity, trust, and relationships.

Stay away from the temptation to share what you don't own. Always defer to and encourage the "owner" of information to pass it along to the intended recipient.

Even if you intentions are well meant—don't communicate in triangles.

ADDITIONAL THOUGHTS ON PROFESSIONAL BUSINESS RELATIONSHIPS

Goal for the Coach: To support the employee in developing business relationships that will support their development.

How do you develop professional business relationships? Today's fast-paced business environments call for informal, personal relationships based on trust and communication. The highest valued professionals will be those who influence, empower, persuade, communicate and work well with others. Informal and virtual networks are the new mode of operation and require well developed interpersonal and communication skills.

In the past, success was based almost exclusively on technical knowledge. Today, the emphasis is on how you manage your relationships and are able to influence and direct those you manage and work with (sometimes they may be in remote locations.)

Some relationships just develop naturally, with very little effort. Sometimes we meet a new colleague and have immediate chemistry with that person.

Chemistry says:

- I like you
- I want to work with you
- We speak the same language

Some relationships take more time and nurturing. There are factors and behaviors that will influence your ability to establish relationships. If you want to develop a relationship, consider the following factors that facilitate relationship building:

DO'S	DO NOT
<ul><li>Engaging others by showing an interest their ideas and participating by sharing yours</li><li>Making "deposits" in the emotional bank account</li><li>Being trustworthy</li><li>Being a thoughtful listener</li><li>Communicating with eye contact</li><li>Using non-verbal body language that signals acceptance</li><li>Being empathetic and understanding</li><li>Engaging your listener by asking questions and sharing the conversation</li><li>Identifying common bonds, similar interests, projects or problems</li></ul>	<ul><li>Act disinterested</li><li>Interrupt people</li><li>"One up" others by competing with them</li><li>Be negative</li><li>Be controlling</li><li>Monopolize</li></ul>

SOME GENERAL TIPS

- Body language communicates in not-so-subtle ways. Gestures and movements send a message about your self-confidence, insecurity, arrogance and many other characteristics.
- Lack of eye contact may indicate a lack of interest, distraction, or insecurity. Continuous eye contact may feel invasive and can create discomfort. Appropriate eye contact is engaging.
- Facial expressions can signal engagement, buy-in, approval and support.
- Animation adds energy and enthusiasm to your message.
- Listening puts the other at ease by conveying interest in their ideas. Key listening activities include:
  - Receiving the message by focusing on the speaker, their words and their ideas
  - Processing the message by thinking about the message and pondering the meaning rather than thinking about your next turn to talk
  - Responding to the message validates that you have heard the message
  - "Mirroring" the message is equally effective means to convey that you have heard the message

HOW TO MAINTAIN PROFESSIONAL RELATIONSHIPS

In order to maintain professional relationships, you need to be attentive to them and nurture them. Stephen Covey calls this "making deposits" into the emotional bank account. The important fundamental rules of healthy professional relationships include:

- You keep confidences; you can be trusted.
- You keep sensitive information in the "the vault"; you coach colleagues through sensitive issues and keep it between you.
- You follow through on promises and commitments.
- You speak favorably about your colleagues –publicly and privately.
- You honestly address conflicts and try to resolve them; you do not ignore them, hoping they will go away.
- You provide and share information that is important and needed for your colleague to be successful.
- If you made an error and embarrassed a colleague and hurt their ego, dignity or reputation, you apologize—genuinely and immediately.
- You give time and attention to your important professional relationships.

Intangible Characteristic 6:

Displaying Professional Image and Presence

The three components that comprise Professional Image and Presence are appearance, demeanor, and style. All three are important to your overall professional reputation. Visual presentation, appearance and your manner and style make immediate and lasting impressions. Do not discount the importance of this intangible.

"Dress the part unless you don't want it!"
--Kenneth Cole

Case Study on Appearance and Demeanor

Dan is a Human Resources Manager for an International Hospitality company. Dan has been in his position for 5 years and is eager for a promotion. Dan is overweight and has not replaced his wardrobe since gaining weight. His clothing is ill fitting and unprofessional. Dan keeps thinking why make the investment in new clothing when I know I will lose weight. Dan is a fun guy who at times can become a little loud and boorish. For example, at an employee luncheon he told several inappropriate jokes. He is not the smoothest person on the team, but that's just who he is. If Dan were told that the promotion is not forthcoming because of what he would consider superficial "cosmetic" reasons, he would be furious.

Dan: The work I do is high quality. What does professional image and presence have to do with my success?

NOTE: Physical appearance is a first professional impression. Is your appearance and demeanor professional?

Complete the following questions to determine to what degree you are aware of the importance of Professional Image to your career success.

Answer the following questions on a scale from "1" to "5" with "1" being low, indicating you could improve your professional image and "5" being high, indicating you are professionally well appointed. This will help to clarify and make you aware of your level of appearance and demeanor.

Do you dress for success?	1	2	3	4	5
Do you "look" the role? Look at successful people in your company. How are they dressed?	1	2	3	4	5
Are you professionally groomed?	1	2	3	4	5
Are your clothes pressed, well fitting, and tasteful?	1	2	3	4	5
Are the fabrics of good quality?	1	2	3	4	5
Is your style clean, crisp, and not flashy?	1	2	3	4	5
Could your appearance be improved by a different hairstyle or different style of clothes?	1	2	3	4	5
Could your appearance be improved if you lost weight and exercised?	1	2	3	4	5

Are you loud? Do you disturb those around you?	1	2	3	4	5
Are you coarse? Do you make unprofessional comments in public?	1	2	3	4	5
Does your joking get in the way of professional discussion?	1	2	3	4	5

NOTE ON PROFESSIONAL WARDROBES

It isn't necessary to totally replace your existing wardrobe. And you needn't make your wardrobe so conservative that it is uninteresting—you can still bring individuality to your way of dressing. Also, you can dress professionally while maintaining your budget. You needn't spend exorbitant sums to look polished. Have a trusted friend or colleague that is a wardrobe "role model" take you on a shopping field trip.

Case Study on Style and Manner

Susan is a manager in a Manufacturing Company. Most recently, she has started attending meetings with the directors and executives of the company. Susan is eager to contribute in the meetings. She sometimes interrupts others when she has a really good idea. She has been, on occasion, known to monopolize the conversation with lengthy, rambling statements. She also has a tendency to be openly honest and sometimes critical of ideas expressed in meetings. Her ideas are spontaneous.

Susan: I thought I would be nervous in these meetings, but I am comfortable. I think I am really contributing to the discussion.

Complete the following questions to determine to what degree you are aware of the importance of Professional Style in your career.

Answer the following questions by rating on a scale from "1" to "5" with "1" being low, indicating you need to be aware and work on your style and "5" being high, indicating your style is appropriate and professional.

Do you regularly contribute to discussions in meetings?	1 2 3 4 5
Do you research, prepare and plan before participating in a client or business meeting?	1 2 3 4 5
Do you understand the protocols of meeting participation? Do you understand what your role will be in a meeting?	1 2 3 4 5
Are you a clear communicator—to the point, crisp and succinct?	1 2 3 4 5
Do you demonstrate maturity, flexibility and seasoned judgment?	1 2 3 4 5
Do you have a "filter" to stop inappropriate comments and do you use it?	1 2 3 4 5
Do you listen first, prepare thoughts and then express ideas?	1 2 3 4 5

	1	2	3	4	5
Are you confident without being "cocky" when communicating?	1	2	3	4	5
Are you sensitive and careful not to publicly challenge or confront other's ideas and thoughts, but instead query others in a consultative manner to get information while affording them to the opportunity to make a counter-point?	1	2	3	4	5
Are you sensitive to not humiliate or criticize those in the meeting or those outside the meeting?	1	2	3	4	5
Are you careful not to regularly take center stage?	1	2	3	4	5
Do you maintain a healthy engagement with the group?	1	2	3	4	5
Do you exhibit your passion in a rational manner?	1	2	3	4	5
Are you present during meetings? Attentive? Actively listening?	1	2	3	4	5
Do you refrain from texting, using your cell phone or doing other work during meetings?	1	2	3	4	5
Are you on time?	1	2	3	4	5
Do you have personal impact?	1	2	3	4	5

Do you have personal warmth?	1	2	3	4	5
Do you project energy in your pace and physical demeanor?	1	2	3	4	5

Notes on Professional Image and Presence:

NOTE ON THE IMPORTANCE OF MEETING POWER

Meetings and presentations expose you to larger numbers of employees and are situations in which perceptions of your professional reputation get formed. Every time you speak you are being assessed. Listening and processing what you are hearing in a meeting should precede jumping into the discussion.

EXERCISE 18 for the EMPLOYEE

Having read the case study and answered the questions, how would you describe your professional presence? Are there areas for improvement?

EXERCISE 19 for the EMPLOYEE and the COACH

Discuss the results of your self-ratings on appearance, demeanor and style with your Coach. Together, discuss two specific actions that you will take to improve your professional presence:

1. _____

2. _____

Chapter 3

Creating an Individual Development Plan

Why create an Individual Development Plan? An Individual Development Plan supports your personal and professional development by creating a roadmap and step-by-step plan to support change. Here is the fascinating approach that Benjamin Franklin used:

Modern psychologists recognize three key elements in Benjamin Franklin's three-hundred-year-old procedure for changing habits:

1. He started out committed to the new behaviors.
2. He worked on only one habit at a time.
3. He put in place visual reminders.

Forbes Magazine, January 1, 2013
Pat Brans, Contributor

BEHAVIORAL CHANGE

Before creating your development plan, let's briefly take a look at how people make behavioral changes.

Technical development, as mentioned previously, generally refers to a tangible competency. For example, if I, in fact, need to enhance my understanding of Behavioral Interviewing, I can take a class that will teach me the fundamentals of Behavioral Interviewing. And then I can practice this skill with an experienced recruiter and finally go off on my own and interview. It is not so with intangibles. Your approach and development plan will differ considerably when you work on these areas because to change behaviors requires ongoing thought, commitment, practice and feedback.

The following is a change model that spells out how behavioral change occurs:

- Step 1: **Being Aware**—you have received <u>and</u> solicited feedback in the areas where change may be required. You have completed and answered the questions on intangibles honestly. You have shared your self-assessment of your intangible development needs with your Coach or Mentor (if you have one).

- Step 2: **Accepting the Feedback**—You have accepted (not denied, defended or argued) that change is needed and change will support your professional success. You recognize that not changing your behavior may cause your career to stall or derail.

- Step 3: **Being Motivated to Change**—change cannot be forced upon you, you must decide that there is a compelling reason to change that will positively impact your career.

- Step 4: **Creating a Plan**—You are committed to changing and will create a specific development plan that will support you in behavioral change.

- Step 5: **Taking Action**—You will commit to executing the goals set in your development plan. You will take the initiative to ensure that you will change and others will observe the change. You will take charge of your career and advancement in appropriate ways by developing advocates, identifying role models, using your coach, mentor and informal mentor.

Whom to Solicit Feedback from:

1. Do you have at least two people you can trust to give you honest feedback?
2. Do you have two people who are at a higher level than you who would be willing to provide you with honest feedback if you shared your self-assessment?
3. Do you have a trusted peer who you can confide in?
4. Remember that honest feedback can be tough to hear, and even tougher to give.
5. Who are the resources to support you as you execute you development plan?

THE DEVELOPMENT PLAN (SAMPLE)

SMART is a widely used acronym for creating goals. Smart goals should be specifically stated and include activities and actions that can be measured and realistically be completed in a timely manner. Following is a sample SMART Goal that supports the Intangible around developing and sustaining strong relationships and networks.

The SMART acronym stands for:

Specific

Measurable

Achievable

Realistic

Timely

Specific	Intangible	Measurable	Timely
Develop and strengthen relationships outside of my department	RELATIONSHIPS	1. Meet with my mentor to review the company's organization chart 2. Identify 7 to 10 peers who are successful in their careers and at building relationships 3. Invite 10 peers to lunch to get to know them 4. Prior to meeting, prepare my personal introduction, devise questions to ask them about their roles and career path with the company	1. In Mid-May 2. Mid-May 3. Invite 1 peer per month over next 10 months 4. Prepare for meetings and meet with your Mentor to discuss approach and strategy

The Achievable and Realistic components of the goal should be discussed with the boss to determine the viability of achieving the goal based on the changing needs of the business and your responsibilities.

Chapter 4

Additional Coaching Topics

The following chapter provides additional information for the Coach on intangible characteristics as they guide and mentor their employees.

Topics include:

1. Mentoring

2. Role Models

3. Professional Reputation

4. Behavioral Change

5. Repairing Damaged Relationships

COACHING TOPICS

MENTORING

For the Coach: How can you support the employee in selecting and utilizing a mentor?

Questions:

- How does the employee identify a Mentor?
- How should the employee use a Mentor?
- How can the employee get the benefits of having a mentor if you don't have a formal Mentor Program in your company?

Many organizations do not have formal Mentoring Programs. Typically, formal mentor programs are based upon one-on-one relationships where a less-experienced employee is matched with a seasoned and experienced Manager or Executive who has the technical or non-technical skills that are specific to supporting the areas where the individual needs to grow and develop.

The purpose of a Mentoring relationship is for the mentor to share knowledge and support the individual in the development of their professional and personal skills. The Mentor may also provide support in career development and individual development and goal planning.

Many companies have formal mentoring programs as a part of their professional development initiatives. Formal mentor programs offer structure, guidelines, and most importantly, an agreed upon outcome for meetings. Mentors generally meet with their mentees once a month and establish a time frame. The focus of the meetings is developmental—to learn from a more experienced person.

If the company does not have a formal program, there are alternative ways to get the benefits without being in a formal mentor relationship. Here's how to proceed to get the value of having a mentor:

GETTING STARTED

Identify the intangible characteristic the employee wants to develop to become a stronger professional. For example, is it gaining advocates in the company or expanding their network of relationships? Is it getting senior management to know more about your talents and work? Or is it developing a skill, such as being a more organized, efficient person?

The coach and employee should identify a person at a more senior level who possesses the skill, competency, or intangible the employee wishes to develop.

When selecting an informal mentor, consider the following questions:

- What does the employee want to gain from the mentoring relationship?
- What skills, styles or talents does the employee want to develop (technical or non-technical)?
- Is there a potential manager who demonstrates those skills, styles or talents?
- Is there a particular person in the company who has a fresh perspective and objective opinion the employee would like to seek and understand?

CREATING MEETING TOPICS

Identify business and development topics to discuss when meeting with a formal or informal mentor. Below are some sample topics that might be addressed during meeting:

- State the purpose for meeting, e.g., you have great networking skills I would like to learn from you. How did you gain comfort and poise in meeting people and selling yourself?
- Ask for their thoughts on what it takes to succeed professionally.
- Discuss current projects and daily challenges, as well as current career and development goals and issues.
- Ask for advice on how to effectively communicate with managers and executives.
- Seek out ideas on how to improve performance.
- Discuss career paths and concerns.

INTRODUCING YOURSELF TO A MENTOR

Prepare a brief introduction of your background. Make certain the mentor is aware of your current roles and responsibilities.

As an introduction to the mentor, prepare a list of professional information that could possibly be discussed during the meeting. The meeting will be more useful and comfortable if the mentee is prepared for the conversation:

- University/major
- Hometown
- Prior work experience
- Professional development goals
- Long-term career goals
- Greatest personal accomplishment
- Outside activities, interests, hobbies

MAKING CONTACT

Introduce yourself by calling or emailing the mentor to request a brief meeting. (Or ask an advocate for an introduction.) Before meeting, prepare a statement about the purpose of the meeting and why they were selected, such as, "I have always been impressed by your ability to make great presentations and would appreciate a few minutes of your time to discuss how you became such a terrific speaker." People are generally flattered to be recognized in this way and will usually accommodate a meeting.

The employee may have more than one informal mentor. But don't overdo this process—maybe meet with one new manager over a 2-3 month period. Avoid being the person who is constantly calling executives and taking their time. (Refer to the section on "Organizational Savvy.")

ROLE MODELS

<u>Goal for the Coach</u>: Help the employee understand the importance of role models and the impact they can have on one's career.

What is a role model?

A role model is an individual who is admired and respected for qualities, characteristics, skills, style or a variety of personal and professional attributes. Psychology studies indicate that most of us have consciously or unconsciously used role models throughout our lives, and that aspects of our personality come from the integration of the aspects of these people. The psychological term "imprinting" is also used to describe the observance of others' behaviors and making them a part of our essence.

A role model is similar to a mentor in terms of the employee's respect for them as an individual who is more skilled or experienced. Whereas a mentor relationship is interactive, the employee needn't necessarily have an active relationship with a role model. Simple observation and imitation of role models makes an individual a stronger professional and provides living examples of ways to act in a more professional manner. For example, you will probably never meet Bill Gates or Warren Buffet personally, but by reading about them, reading what they have written, hearing them speak, learning their stories of success and philosophies for success may have a positive impact on you as a current or future leader.

PROFESSIONAL REPUTATION

Goal for the Coach: To help the employee to understand how others perceive them in the workplace.

What is a professional reputation and why is it important to understand how others perceive you? How can you find out how you are perceived?

After attending many performance review meetings where managers discuss employee talents and development needs and decide whether to promote employees, I have come to conclude the importance of one's professional relationship. Generally these discussions are based upon measurable and tangible outcomes of the employee's performance over the past year, such as "Bill completed the IT conversion in a timely manner" or "Susan received many accolades from the client on the systems integration." In addition to their accomplishments, there will frequently be a discussion of the employee's intangible characteristics that may support or deny a promotion. These perceived characteristics plus technical expertise equate to a person's "professional reputation."

PROFESSIONAL REPUTATIONS

Here are a few positive and negative characteristics of a professional reputation that may surface regarding performance:

POSITIVES	NEGATIVES
• Takes initiative • Comes to me with solutions, not just problems • Goes beyond expectations • Does whatever it takes • Is committed to the company • Has self-confidence • Is a great problem solver • Makes the most of limited resources • Has high energy and is optimistic • Is trustworthy • Is professional in all manners—appearance, presentation, etc. • Is highly likeable; people want to work with them	• Lacks initiative • Does the minimum to get by • Isn't involved in company activities; doesn't appear to be committed to the company • Lacks self-confidence • Talks too much in meetings; sometimes inappropriately • Never participates in discussions • Is negative and speaks negatively about company policies, initiatives, people • Has alienated folks; people don't want to work with them • Is arrogant

All of the above characteristics contribute to the professional reputation. A professional reputation is powerful and can support or break long-term career success.

If the employee wants a true picture of how they are perceived by management, there are several ways to gain this information. The employee and coach should work together to determine the strategy Here's how to begin:

- Identify a trusted person who will be candid and truthful about how they perceive your strengths and weakness. This could be a boss, coach, mentor, advocate, or colleague.

- Recognize that asking for feedback is a huge favor and show respect and appreciation to those who provide honest feedback that you can use for your professional development.

- Position your request for feedback in a manner that is non-threatening to the person you are asking.

- Make your request less threatening by asking them for feedback on your total reputation—both the positive and the not so positive. What are your strengths as they see them? What are some of your development needs? Make certain not to ask for the source of this information. This is strictly for your personal and professional improvement and development.

- If negative feedback is a total surprise, don't become defensive but do recognize this is most likely a "blind spot."

CHANGING PERCEPTIONS

- Identify what needs to change. Be specific.
- What does it look like now?
- How will it look after I change?
- Who will notice?
- What will they notice?

- Ask your coach or mentor, would you be willing to provide me with feedback when you observe these negative behaviors?

BEHAVIORAL CHANGE

<u>Goal for the Coach:</u> How to coach the employee on changing behavior.

When change is needed which is behavioral, not technical, how does one make the change?

Behavioral change is different from learning or enhancing a skill. Behavioral change is similar to breaking a habit.   Breaking a habit always requires awareness and then commitment on the part of the employee. This is what we know about changing a behavior:

- You must be aware of and accept that change is needed. This is difficult, as many of us prefer not to receive negative feedback. So first and foremost, accept the feedback
- Digest the feedback. You may need time to accept the information, especially if it was a "blind spot," something you were not aware of.
- Appreciate the feedback. Thank the feedback giver. We cannot develop if we are in the dark about our weaknesses
- Determine your readiness and openness to change. If you aren't ready, you won't change.
- People are generally motivated to change because of internal or external forces—what are yours? Will change bring more respect, more responsibility, higher self-worth, a promotion, a salary increase?
- Behavioral change is not the same as skill development.
- Behavioral change is never easy or comfortable.
- Behavioral change can be slow and is generally not linear; relapses will occur.

- Behavioral change does not occur in a vacuum—ongoing feedback mechanisms and support are critical to sustain your ability to change.
- Identify a "change" agent—who sees you in the work environment and can support you in your desire to change by providing you with real-time feedback.
- Recognize that your behavior impacts your future.

REPAIRING DAMAGED PROFESSIONAL RELATIONSHIPS

Goal for the Coach: Provide guidance to an employee who has had a conflict with a peer or superior.

How do I repair a damaged professional relationship?

In repairing a professional relationship, you need to start with analysis. Some steps for repairing damaged professional relationships begin with thinking through the situation and considering the following:

EMOTIONAL BANK ACCOUT

Do you have an emotional bank account with this person? If so, you already have an established relationship. Even with the bank account, you will still need to extend an apology, and express a desire to discuss the event with mutual agreement about going forward.

Occasionally, we damage a relationship without being aware that we have. This is a great learning opportunity to rethink our behavior not only with this relationship, but perhaps with all business relationships. For example, we may not realize we took credit for another's ideas or shared personal information that we assumed was public.

ANALYZE THE EVENT

What triggered the event? You may not be aware of what triggered the event and if that is the situation, you might begin the conversation by stating, "I sense that things are strained between us and I hope I haven't in some way offended or embarrassed you. Please help me understand what has happened." If you are truly unaware, this will provide an opportunity to have an objective conversation, appropriate apology and agreement about behavior going forward.

If you are aware of the damage you have caused, you will want to determine if this was a single event or a pattern. For example, are you consistently critical, competitive, or disrespectful? What has your role been in this situation?

EMPATHIZE

Think empathetically—be open to understanding your colleague's viewpoint. Listen to what your colleague is saying and ask clarifying questions. Try not to be defensive, but do provide information that will help your colleague to understand your position. In discussing the situation, you may reach an impasse and think that you are misunderstood. Your colleague may also feel misunderstood. But in professional relationships, both your success and your colleague's depend on a collaborative relationship. Therefore, it is of utmost importance to come to some resolution.

STEPHEN COVEY'S ADVICE

In Stephen Covey's book *The Seven Habits of Highly Effective People* he discusses the three possible outcomes of conflict resolution:

<u>Win-Lose</u> one person will win; the other will lose

<u>Lose-Lose</u> we can't agree and we can't compromise so we will leave the issue unresolved and possibly harbor negative feelings and a forever-changed relationship

<u>Win-Win or No Deal</u> requires maturity on the part of both parties; a desire to move forward and willingness to compromise. Agreement to work until we find a satisfactory solution we can both live with

OUTLINE FOR MEETING

Some tips on the meeting (you may want the other person to read these tips as well before you meet):
   a. Request to meet in a private and neutral place
   b. Express the desire for a win-win solution
   c. Listen first and then respond
   d. Don't drill down into minute details—focus on a positive result
   e. Treat your colleague with respect
   f. Try not to be judgmental
   g. Keep emotions in check

h. Self-disclose, be honest, apologize if you were wrong
i. Be flexible
j. Use diplomacy and honesty
k. Work objectively, not emotionally
l. Once you reach an agreement, you should discuss how to go forward

Chapter 5

Coaching on Five <u>Tangible</u> Competencies

This chapter provides additional tips for coaching. These five tangible competencies are frequently discussed in the context of professional development .

1. Communication

2. Organization

3. Time Management

4. Delegation

5. Confidence

Coaching to Improve **COMMUNICATION**

The following checklists can be used to provide the Coach and Employee with an awareness of whether they are an effective communicator. Remember, communication is behavioral, and as stated earlier, requires awareness to remedy.

<u>INEFFECTIVE</u> COMMUNICATORS MAY HAVE THESE BEHAVIORS:

- Do not give clear instructions on roles, responsibilities, expectations
- Are not clear; are misunderstood by others
- Are not good at communicating a project plan
- Get stressed because of information overload
- Miss deadlines
- Don't understand what they are supposed to be doing
- Haven't listened closely
- Are fidgety and distracted
- Interrupt people before they have completed their thoughts
- Ramble on and go off on a tangent
- Talk around the sensitive issues rather than being direct
- Don't provide all the facts necessary to get the job done
- Believe they know it all and don't need to listen to others
- Procrastinate in giving "bad news"
- Don't follow through
- Don't keep team members informed

EFFECTIVE COMMUNICATORS USE THESE TECHNIQUES

- Provide/ask for a clear definition of roles, responsibilities, and expectations
- Take notes on key points in discussion around expectations and timelines
- Keep subordinates motivated and empowered by defining their roles and responsibilities
- Discuss their communication preferences. Do you prefer email, voicemail, or drop in?
- Provide "executive" briefings by summarizing the key points and excluding superfluous details
- Ask about deadlines—when is the project due? Will there be check-in times? When? What is the timeline?
- Are trusted as a part of the team because they provide the team with information they need to do a good job
- Ensure that tasks get done right the first time because the expectations were clearly stated
- Are seen by clients and co-workers as a "go-to" person who will respond in a timely manner with good information
- Meet deadlines
- Keep all well informed of the progress and status of projects
- Ensure that everyone gains a greater understanding and knowledge of issues or obstacles that may impact the work
- Ensure that there are no surprises on evaluations
- Are attentive to needs, questions, and concerns
- Communicate difficult issues and provide constructive criticism effectively
- Communicate positive feedback early and often

HOW TO DEVELOP STRONG COMMUNICATION SKILLS

- Build rapport with colleagues by finding common ground, e.g., interests, values, etc.
- Listen with intention to other people
- Ask questions to clarify
- Try to understand the other person's point of view
- Respond directly to issues
- Be specific. Pinpoint the key topics you wish to discuss. Speak clearly.
- Keep your messages simple
- Ask for feedback, input and insights from others
- Be positive and enthusiastic
- Avoid distractions—Blackberry, cell phone, texts, and calls on your office phone during meetings

Coaching to Improve **ORGANIZATION**

The following checklists can be used to provide you with an awareness of whether you are effective at organizing your work and your life—an essential skill for success.

DISORGANIZED INDIVIDUALS MAY HAVE THESE BEHAVIORS

- They get overwhelmed and frustrated because they can't find things.
- Their work does not look professional.
- They spend unnecessary time looking for things.
- They work longer hours to get less completed.
- They can't access or find the resources they need to do the work.
- They are not as efficient as they could be.
- They don't keep their calendar up to date and sometimes miss internal and external deadlines.
- Their disorganization may impact the work of others.
- Their disorganization makes it difficult for their boss and colleagues to do a good job.
- They spin their wheels.
- Their office space looks unprofessional, sloppy.
- The quality and quantity of their performance may be impacted.

ORGANIZED INDIVIDUALS HAVE THESE ADVANTAGES

- They know where to find things.
- They are able to access materials, quickly .
- They have better control of their schedules and calendar.
- They are better able to multi-task.
- They better utilize their time.

- They accomplish and get more done.
- They are able to meet deadlines.
- They are less stressed.
- They generally have better overall performance.
- Their office space looks professional and organized.

HOW TO BECOME BETTER ORGANIZED

- Identify someone who is organized and ask them to help you organize your space, time, calendar, projects.
- Delegate work, if and when appropriate.
- Set objectives and goals with specific times and dates on your calendar.
- Break large projects into reasonable steps.
- Outline projects from beginning to end. Ask the questions who, what, where, when and how on each line of the outline.
- Maximize the use of technology.
- Read a book on organization skills or project management.

Coaching to Improve **TIME MANAGEMENT SKILLS**

<u>INEFFECTIVE</u> TIME MANAGERS MAY HAVE THESE BEHAVIORS

- They are stressed.
- They feel like they always have too many balls in the air.
- They are buried with a mountain of details.
- They are frustrated because they aren't accomplishing as much as they would like to.
- They seem to "lose" time and don't know where it goes.
- They don't finish work as quickly as they would like to.
- They feel that people are "taking" their time.

<u>EFFECTIVE</u> TIME MANAGERS HAVE THE FOLLOWING BEHAVIORS

- They are less stressed.
- They have control over their calendar.
- They complete projects and tasks as scheduled.
- They have increased productivity and efficiency.
- They increase the amount of time to focus energy on the more interesting/higher quality work.

HOW TO MORE EFFECTIVELY MANAGE YOUR TIME

- Are you using the Cloud and other tools that are available to help you manage your time?
- Are you effectively delegating?
- Learn to say "no"
- Have someone help you organize your files-- paper and computer

- Are you setting goals?
- Are you setting deadlines?
- Are you creating action steps to achieve your goals?
- Identify someone in the firm who is really good at time management. Ask them to meet with you to review a typical day's calendar and share their techniques for successful time management.
- Review your social patterns. Are you spending too much time in social situations? Visiting and talking about non-work items?
- Know when and how to close a conversation.
- Be sensitive to interruptions--yours and others. Find a comfortable and diplomatic way to tell people that you cannot be interrupted at this time
- At the end of the day, review your accomplishments and create a list of what you need to do the following day

Coaching to Improve **DELEGATION SKILLS**

<u>INEFFECTIVE</u> DELEGATORS MAY HAVE THESE CONCERNS AND FRUSTRATIONS

- You feel stretched. You don't have enough time to complete all of your work.
- You're stressed most of the time.
- You're doing your own job and that of five other people.
- You have less time to focus on what's important in your job.
- You aren't growing professionally, because you're stuck doing all the jobs you did before you were promoted <u>and</u> your new job as well.
- You're resentful because you don't believe that others are helping out as much as they could be and should be.
- You just aren't as effective as you know you could be.

<u>EFFECTIVE</u> DELEGATORS HAVE HIGHER EFFICIENCY AND LESS STRESS

- For the most part, you will be able to focus on work that is most appropriate for your level in the organization.
- You won't be doing everything by yourself.
- Your staff will be clear about the role they play and how to work with you and other staff members.
- Your staff will become more participative and utilized.
- Your staff will develop professionally.
- You will develop professionally.
- You and your staff will all be more effective.
- You and your staff will all be more productive.
- You and your staff will all be more professionally satisfied.

HOW DO YOU BECOME AN EFFECTIVE DELEGATOR?

- Let go of being a perfectionist and a person who controls everything. Delegating requires letting go.
- Realize that when you must control all of the work, you deprive others of having new experiences to learn the skills you already know.
- If you are a new supervisor, recognize that you may be managing or delegating to people who used to be your peers. Acknowledge it and work together with them to establish a new working relationship. Define the new roles and responsibilities while building on the respect of the previous relationship.
- Begin to trust that others can learn and be as effective as you are but recognize that they will need your guidance, support, permission and empowerment to get there.
- Create a plan.
- Clearly and openly communicate roles, responsibilities and expectations.
- Help others figure it out and let them figure it out. Encourage your staff to work on solving business problems--but keep the door open and offer your support as a resource.
- Engage your staff. Solicit their ideas--"This is our project...how can we all contribute?"
- Identify someone inside or outside your organization who has perfected the art of delegating, Use this person as a role model. Study them. Interview them. Ask them to be a resource when you are problem-solving issues around delegation.
- Yes, you can probably do the job faster and better by yourself, but realize that holding on to that work will prevent you from becoming a good manager and prevent your staff from growing and learning.

Coaching to Increase **SELF-CONFIDENCE**

WHEN YOU LACK SELF CONFIDENCE YOU MAY APPEAR LESS COMPETENT THAN YOU ARE BECAUSE

- You are unsure of what you are doing.
- You need a lot of reassurance.
- You doubt yourself.
- You put yourself down.
- You don't feel comfortable approaching senior managers or clients directly.
- You lack self confidence in front of more senior people.
- You appear nervous and tense.
- You don't take risks.
- You hide your mistakes.
- You are afraid to express the good ideas you may have.

WHEN YOU ARE SELF CONFIDENT YOU DISPLAY DIFFERENT BEHAVIORS

- You can introduce yourself to others at associations, community events, etc. types of meetings comfortably.
- You present yourself and your ideas with ease.
- You make eye contact.
- You "speak up" when you have a good idea.
- You feel comfortable asking the questions you need to ask to do a good job.
- You are certain about your ability to generally make good decisions.
- You are willing to share your ideas.
- You are comfortable around senior people.
- You take risks.
- Clients and colleagues ask you for your suggestions.

- Colleagues respect your opinions; peers trust you and your technical abilities.
- You are able to demonstrate to people how good you really are at your job.

TECHNIQUES FOR GAINING SELF-CONFIDENCENE

- Ask your manager to help you to create a development plan that focuses on the skills you need to master to perform well in your current position. The better your performance, the more confident you will feel.
- Ask for feedback. Don't wait for feedback to come to you. "How was my presentation in the staff meeting? What suggestions do you have for helping me prepare for the next time?"
- Study people who project confidence. What behaviors do they demonstrate?
- Raise your hand to do a completely new type of assignment or work (sometimes called a "stretch" assignment). New assignments take us out of our comfort zone, force us to take risks and elevate our self-confidence. Make sure that you ask for the support that you need to be successful.
- Volunteer to speak at meetings.
- Volunteer to manage a project.
- Seek out support and resources who will help you to succeed.

As a Coach, you can support an individual in developing self-confidence when you:

- Realize that the plan you create with the employee will need to be very specific and individualized.
- Be sensitive as to how you provide constructive criticism. Make sure that when mistakes are made, you coach the employee to learn from them--not punish them.
- Never criticize an employee in front of others. Give feedback privately.
- Praise the employee when you see them demonstrating positive behaviors. Acknowledge their successes.

Chapter 6

The Coach's Library

FYI—For Your Improvement
Michael M Lombardo and Robert W. Eichinger
Copyright © 1996-2
2009, Lominger International: a Korn/Ferry Co.

FYI is a quick reference guide for development and coaching. It is a useful tool for managers, mentors, and feedback givers. The book lists 67 competencies, 10 performance dimensions and 19 career stoppers with checklists to determine if you are skilled, unskilled or overusing a skill. Each competency has 10 remedies for development.

The Trusted Advisor
David Maister
Copyright © 2000, Free Press

The theme of this book is that the key to professional success is not just technical mastery of one's discipline, but also the ability to work with clients and colleagues in such a way as to earn their trust and gain their confidence.

The Likability Factor
Tim Sanders
Copyright © 2005, 2006, Three Rivers Press

Likable people bring out the best in others, get recognized and outperform others. Four elements of likability include: friendliness, relevance, empathy and realness. This book provides information on how to raise your likability factor.

Leading Change
John P. Cotter
Copyright © 2006, John P. Cotter
> *A classic leadership book that describes the 8-stage process to lead a successful cultural change initiative from establishing urgency to supporting new approaches in the workplace.*

Now, Discover Your Strengths
Marcus Buckingham
Copyright © 2001, The Gallup Organization
> *This book describes what is required to have a successful career by discovering your strengths and building and focusing on them.*

Type Talk at Work: How the 16 Personality Types Determine Your Success on the Job
Otto Kroeger
Copyright © 2002, Dell Publishing
> *This book is an introduction to Myers-Briggs which is a personality preference tool that describes 16 personality preference types and how individuals make decisions, collect data and prefer communicating. This is an excellent tool for understanding your boss, teammates, peers and self.*

Learning to Lead: A Workbook on Becoming a Leader
Warren Bennis & Joan Goldsmith
Copyright © 2010, Basic Book
> *This book contains self-assessments and interactive skill-building exercises to gain insight into true leadership.*

First, Break All the Rules: What the World's Greatest Managers do Differently
Marcus Buckingham
Copyright © 1999, Simon & Schuster
> *The "four keys" to becoming an excellent manager: finding the right fit for your employees; focusing on their strengths; defining the right expectations and results; and selecting staff for talent—not just knowledge and skills.*

Execution: The Discipline of Getting Things Done
Larry Bossidy and Ram Charan
Copyright © 2002, Crown Business
> *This book describes the real and practical job of being successful. It stresses the importance of being passionately engaged in an organization and encourages robust and honest communication about people, strategy and operations.*

The First 90 Days: Critical Success Strategies for New Leaders at All Levels
Michael Watkins
Copyright © 2003, Harvard Business School Publishing
> *This book lays out a framework for successfully integrating into a new job. It stresses having clear expectations, roles and responsibilities, alignment with the boss and building trusting relationships.*

What Got You Here Won't Get You There: How Successful People Become Even More Successful
By Marshall Goldsmith
Copyright © 2011, Writers of the Round Table Press
> *The author describes 20 bad habits that can potentially derail a successful career. Most are behavioral problems and he recommends humorous and effective solutions for change.*

Difficult Conversations: How to Discuss What Matters Most
By Stone, Patton and Heen
Copyright © 2007, Penguin Books

> *An extremely useful resource designed by the Harvard Negotiation Project this book walks you through a step-by-step approach for how to have the toughest conversations by staying constructive and focused.*